THE

End of the Beginning

A Collection of Poems

Advanced praise for, *The End of the Beginning*

"In this second complete collection, each poem has its very own current, ferrying the reader to places that are often physically familiar, but emotionally unexplored. This new work blends many of the characteristics that make up great poetry, such as humor in the shadow of suffering, and introspection where there would most commonly be judgement. But best of all, these are poems that are felt before they are fully understood."

—SIMON VAN BOOY, best-selling author of, *Night Came With Many Stars.*

"Intimations abound in poems of weightless memory. Words crisscross subjects from childhood to adulthood, and recover familiar territory, before taking flight into unwritten country."

—LUCAS HUNT, winner of the John Steinbeck Award for Poetry.

"Carrie Voigt Schonhoff's collection is a beautifully stark portrayal of the quiet moments we often overlook in our daily lives. These poems are gorgeous reflections and pauses on what it means to be human, to live through time. Her lines are reminders of this: 'It's not so much the suffering/as it is the silence.' Everyone needs to read this and remind themselves of their own being."

—JOANNA C. VALENTE, author of, *A Love Story* and editor of, *A Shadow Map.*

"Brimming with love, loss, and loneliness—Carrie Voigt Schonhoff's The End of the Beginning *searches for the silver linings—for the light we all hang on to through dark times. Rich with imagery that inspires and instructs,* The End of the Beginning *is a gentle ode to the resiliency in all of us."*

—SARAH JONES, author of, *Lies I Tell Myself.*

THE

END OF THE BEGINNING

A Collection of Poems

CARRIE VOIGT SCHONHOFF

ALSO BY CARRIE VOIGT SCHONHOFF

POETRY
The Liminal Space

For more information, contact:
www.liminalartistry.com
liminalartistryllc@gmail.com
@liminalartistry on Instagram & Twitter

.

First Edition
ISBN
Hard cover: 978-0-578-96688-5
Soft cover: 978-0-578-98566-4

Library of Congress Control Number: 2021919895

Cover art by Sydney Schonhoff

DEDICATIONS

To Grandpa Chuck—thank you for cherishing me
To my daughter Sydney and son Austin—
the best and bravest people I'll ever know

CONTENTS

THE UNION WAY

I finished grouting my bathroom floor
the night of the waxing Hunter's Moon.
As I sealed my amateur work
I remembered Grandpa Chuck,
a tile layer by trade.
He was let go from his job
and promptly had a breakdown.

I have kept mementos of him.
His gold metal union card
still sits on my shelf.
Worth nothing to anyone
it means everything to me.
Beside it is an Easter photo
of us hand-in-hand.
I was young then
and carried his red
bank-issued coin purse
that held enough for a Shirley Temple
and an Old-Fashioned
in Grandpa's favorite *church*
with the high stools.

The rooms of my childhood home
still lined with his handiwork,
make me think of a time when *my* kids
will have only photographs of their mama
along with the odd talisman;
a pen almost out of ink,
an amethyst crystal,
a wedding ring no longer in style,
and of course, this poem.

HEAR THE WIND BLOW

I used to sing *Down in the Valley*
and swing my blonde hair
while perched in the red wagon
behind Dad's tractor,
hauling wood
to the brick hearth,
or for bonfires in a circle of evergreens
planted the year I was born.

When my feet touched the pedals
I got to drive,
but soon jeans were tighter,
hair was bigger,
legs smoother,
it was time to stop singing out loud.

Today, somewhere,
someone,
is belting out
their *Down in the Valley*
while they still can.

SECRETS

We all have them
big and small.
Sometimes to protect ourselves,
sometimes others.
They turn black and white to grey
or end up being fun to pass around
(especially when drunk).

But it's never the whole story
because that would mean
standing in our own truth
which is much harder
than breaking off a piece to share.

XANADU

When I was 13,
sky high on hormones,
I laced up and roller-skated
with my two best friends
in an unfinished basement.

We'd figure-eight exposed poles,
dodge Christmas decorations,
jump power tools.

Always with our favorites:
Kiss on My List
The Tide is High
I'm Alive
Another One Bites the Dust

Turns out that two friends
are better than three.
But it takes only one,
at 51,
with a credit card,
to rent the rink and fly.

COME OUT TO PLAY

Every day he and I would meet
in the middle of our lots.
A ball kept there,
changed over the years.
From sunup to sundown
we would throw and catch
then leave it for another day.
At some point a picnic table appeared,
replaced the ball.
Laughs and stories were shared,
tears were shed,
hands held when needed.
Seems like just a moment ago
we moved away,
to our separate cities.

Alone at my mahogany desk,
I gaze at the worn glove and ball
hoping this poem will land
somewhere precious.

THIS IS WHAT GRIEF LOOKS LIKE

At first, I'd wake up crying,
drenched by light falling
through drape-less windows.
I'd sit up and mumble the Lord's Prayer,
or what I could remember of it,
sure I was more Zen than Catholic.

Then, believing I could cycle
through suffering and rebirth
faster than nature allowed,
I pretended to be a guru
with healing powers
and bracelets stamped with words:
hope, peace, warrior.

Now my eyes and arms are clear—
but the moment life tilts
my thoughts toward the present,
guilt tolls in the distance.

When gone,
my request
is to be forgotten
as soon as possible.

HE COULD BE ANYWHERE

On a trip to the Outer Banks years ago,
we told my young daughter
the friendly seagull's name was Fred.

We fed him cookie parts
and stale bread.

When we left, he followed,
hopping over the sand
and snapping his beak,
goodbye, goodbye, goodbye.

We returned to our beach
in winter after my husband died
and found a lone seagull
dodging scattered feathers.

He squawked *hello, hello, hello.*

I didn't have the heart
to tell my daughter it was impossible
the same bird could greet us twice,
but then again—
he could be anywhere.

THEY KNOW SOMETHING WE DON'T

Even without contraction,
the virus controlled
the way we interacted.
Quiet panic invaded
bucolic towns and big box stores.

The supermarket played
religious pop
as I gathered essentials
including wine, for stress.

Then on my way home
I saw a ranch with horses
rooted in the stillness
of pasture.

SLIM CHANCE

Two orchids were placed
in a southern window,
able to touch
only if they bloomed
in the right direction.

SIGH OF RELIEF

Nothing feels better
than to be spooned
by a softly breathing mate
under a bright full moon
that hangs over
corn tassels
in the western sky.

LOOK CLOSELY

I opened a book to find
a dried flower
between chapters
of a story long forgotten.

Another volume held a birthday card,
from those days of stamps and raised flags.
Now it's just bills, junk mail
and urgent requests for money
from hospitals, politicians—even God.

Some photographs have stuck to pages
as though wishing to become part
of another story,
one with a beginning and an end.

Mystery and paradox abound
if you care to look
in the cluttered and treasured shelves
of our peopled lives.

AN ARIA IS A SOLO

When I was 26
visiting my parents
for Christmas,
I received a 'thank-you' package
from a shopkeeper I knew.
Inside were handcuffs
and a German opera CD
about adulterous love
between a Cornish knight
and an Irish princess.

When I was back home in Dallas
he flew in from Vermont,
rented a car, and showed up
with a trunk full of Stargazer lilies.

He *had* a girlfriend,
so I felt safe in my position.

I was treated to dinner and a nightcap
as thanks for my help
on his catalog of weapons, knives,
and medieval toys.

Years later, when my husband died
I found the package in a drawer,
and put the CD on as I cleaned.

Interesting how opera usually ends in tragedy.

HIRAETH

He drove north,
shucked his bowtie for boots,
clipped on skis,
and pushed out into the white woods.

He heard his breath
and the chuff of blades,
gliding on the snow,
seeing the sun through trees
instead of skyscrapers.

In his youth,
they had real winters,
when rivers turned to ice mid-fall
and people watched the world
through windows
already frozen on the inside.

NIGHT RIDE

How I love a nocturnal trot
in a world of stars and closed eyes.

Hooves clack and echo on the pavement,
no need for the brimmed hat or silver buckle—
but I still wear them; it's what cowgirls do.

It's easy to build a fire,
sometimes even sleep
before sorting the sick cow
from the herd at sunrise.

Sitting upright in a saddle
will always be better
than lying awake
in the corner of a king.

FOR KRIS

The custard cones dripped
while we skipped through
a chalk game of hopscotch,
grown women acting silly
in the park of their youth.

We grabbed the necks
of wooden animals,
mesmerized by brittle music
in the spinning carousel.

Sitting, our crossed legs
were rooted in the grass.
We stayed there for a long time,
held hands,
even though we were not lovers.

As the sun fell and we let go,
it was with a promise,
that if never-together-again
it wouldn't matter.
Even one day like this
is a victory over sadness.

TYPECAST

I bought a refurbished Olivetti typewriter
from a Spaniard,
with cream cover and blue ribbon spools.
I put it in the passenger seat
atop a stack of clean paper,
snapped a sheet into the carriage
and it was ready.
You never know when
the inspiration will strike,
but I don't want to be caught
texting while driving.

TIME FLIES

Monica and I carefully traversed
the gray stone steps
so she could put her feet
in the silvery water
that used to fuel a mill
with a paddlewheel,
(still working but now only for show).

It had been 30 years since
she and her groom posed
at a nearby tree
after saying their vows.
So young and unafraid,
naïve like all of us
who think getting married
is the answer.

She has reached a milestone
I will never experience.
But numbers
aren't what really matter.

At least I have that.

VISITING THE POET IN GERMANY

I see you walking amidst
cobblestones in old parks,
leaves tumbling past wooden benches
with branches of lovers.

I imagine your hand touching
the bricks on churches
that survived fires and wars,
as though held together by prayers.

I hear you talking to the lost
in your healing voice,
knowing they need
to love themselves
more than you could,
but hoping there is a word
that travels to their center
and creates a spark.

FALL

I've been trapped under
many places and things
over time.

They've weighed on me
like anvils.
Even now, shards of memory
litter the floor
and distant voices tell me things
I honestly don't want to hear.

Tonight at dusk
I ran from the house,
tearing past spirits on the porch,
to launch myself from the highest step
into a crisp heap of leaves.

It's not so much the suffering
as it is the silence.

SETTING BOUNDARIES

I miss the wily hen that ran amok
at the intersection of V and Tri-County.
A Rhode Island red strutting
like she owned the fork.
Despite a roasting or freezing day
she was there,
to be counted on.
But sometimes friendships end
for reasons known only to the weather,
and one day she was gone.

BEHIND CLOSED DOORS

One early December night
I took the pups out and heard something,
a distant melancholy.

I put my barking dogs back inside,
grabbed the flashlight
and moved deftly, without thought,
toward the cries
at the edge of a wood.

Inside an aged oak tree,
under the mead moon
I saw an owl peck
its baby to death.

You just never know
who'll go crazy
next.

DEAR DESERT STORM

An old friend found me
after 28 years of silence.
Discovered our paper hearts
in a footlocker,
sealed off from time
and heartbreak.

He was unsure at first,
if we could make new memories,
even though he would have
knocked on all the doors in town
to find mine.

Back then I knew him
as an untouchable soldier.
Under shared stars we wrote letters
when he wasn't running for shelter.

After the war he faded away—
too young to settle down,
thought he could do better
than a pen pal.

CHERRIES

Door County sours are soft.
Pit them gently
with a clean hairpin,
inserted just so.

Those eaten *accidentally*
in haste when picked,
cause an ache.

I'm taking some home to freeze
for a pie I dream
you'll one day deserve.

MICHAEL

You crossed two oceans
and seven states
in your teal Camaro
to make sure I was
writing and calling
from heaven,
not hell on earth
where you had just been.

NEW DIALECTS

I don't want to change the sheets
and rid the cotton of something I need.

Now that you're gone,
there is no snoring concerto
to flood the darkness.

My chin is still rough from your beard,
I finger it like a trophy.
I even miss your standard answers,
each sentence clipped
not a word wasted, ever.

Thank you for holding my face in your hands,
patting my butt as you pass
when I'm making dinner
and you're busy fixing
anything that needs fixing,
inside and out.

Every lover
has a language to teach
and a language to learn.

RED SKY AT NIGHT

The clouds and the setting sun
were the colors sailors dreamed of.

That evening I felt your hand,
even though
you were nowhere
near water,
and many states away.

SPRING PARADOX

My favorite room in the house
when alone,
is just one of the places
I wish you were with me.

FIORELLI'S FIGURES

If Vesuvius suddenly erupted,
would you flee, gasping,
strangled from the fire and ash?

Or would you spend
those last moments
in someone's arms?

…silent and tangled
for all to see.

TURN THE PAGE

I slid the worn strap over my shoulder,
pulled a pick from the fretboard,
and tuned half a step down
to take advantage of the sharper chords.

But then all at once I placed my palm
on the taught strings,
realizing silence
might be the most memorable note.

WISH I COULD STAY

I will become the ultimate fantasy.
Breathing life into your skin
with my dulcet tones,
I will wash away
questions on your lips.

Promises will not be broken,
perfect meals *will* be served.

Nights will not be quiet.

Nor forgettable.

I am a siren
kissing the back of your neck,
so you'll believe
anything is possible.

It's easier this way—
lust doesn't keep score
the way heartbreak does.

THE EMPTY NEST

I found myself in the wake
of a meandering couple.

The man followed their dog
at the water's edge,
while his wife trailed,
espadrilles in one hand,
shells in the other.

As an early star appeared
behind rows of condos,
they were farther and further apart.
I thought then about how many people
we need in life,
to make up for the one never found
(or lost).

GENERATIONS OF WOMEN

I tried a dress bought on impulse,
but was uncomfortable
in the body that still belongs to me.

So many wasted years believing
it wasn't good enough,
a barrier to being cherished.

ARACHNOPHOBIA

Untether,
and run,
before you become
my last meal.

DATE NIGHT

On Friday nights in winter
the refrigerator stares back,
chimes when I can't decide.
Herbs pose like frail visitors
to my unattended garden.
Bruised peaches
and blackberries,
lifeless in the crisper.
But somehow we all hang on,
waiting to be chosen.

ST. AUGUSTINE CRUSH

Your ancient fort is still black
from the gunpowder of strangers,
their ships once lured
to the pristine beach,
just like us.

We visited in deep summer.
I bought a hat and a cream cotton top.
We shared a Cuban sandwich.

But the shops full of sea glass
and the cracked cobblestone
should have been a warning;
I wouldn't be the first
to be broken slowly
over time.

NARCISSUS

I'm glad you're in love
with yourself.

Saves one of us
the trouble.

TO THE SON SHE COULDN'T KEEP

In freezing Philadelphia,
as I passed the LOVE sculpture,
fountain mist blessed the hand
on my growing belly,
knowing our togetherness
would be temporary,
but our love forever.

You were never unwanted,
only unplanned.

Unable to carry you
beyond the womb,
in this life,
I'm giving you to the couple
that will drive through a snowstorm at night,
to a stranger in labor,
so that you understand
how to find love someday,
and have the courage to keep it.

GOODBYE SERGEANT

Every day I woke
with a weapon affixed to my body.
Each unholy night
brushed teeth
and drank warm water
with the others.

On my last patrol
I found an I.E.D.
with my name,
in blood.

Camouflage failed
with an enemy
I'd never met.

If I'm moving to the astral plane,
or somewhere we can't imagine,
at least part of me still lives
in the eyes of a boy
who will always be waiting in Iowa.

A VACATION CABIN UP NORTH

That first night,
gaming kept my son awake
long enough to catch—in one full breath,
dawn misting the trees.

Later, as I made coffee,
he showed me the picture on his phone,
deep, rich colors not found
in crayon boxes or online games,
but rather a landscape that must be lived,
where there are many characters,
but each has only one life.

TRAVELS WITH DR. CRICHTON

I landed my favorite book at the airport for $8.50.
By 23,000 feet I was enamored
though never able to spell
the author's last name.

That's love for you.

Michael was taller than most men,
a traveler on foot and in the mind,
a doctor and dinosaur enthusiast.

In my thirties
I actually wrote him a letter,
but never mailed it.
This is one of my few regrets.

His death took me by surprise,
I'd pegged him as immortal
or at least permanent,
like my cherished Cambrian fossil
and distant landscapes.

Now in my fifties, I gaze at his headshot
which takes up the entire back cover.
Together, in silence,
Michael and I contemplate pandemics,
share ideas on how to survive everything,
not just meteorites and cancer.

THE WORLD SPINS ONE WAY

I docked at the shore of the Key,
my hair long like before.
I wore the white shirt
because I knew you'd recognize it.

Outside our former haunt
I smelled your cigar
through open windows.
How many nights
did we talk for hours
until the chickens ran
down the street at dawn?

Surprised to see me, you stood,
so very tall.

I'd forgotten *how* tall.

We had everything to say
but went our separate ways
without ever looking back.

The world spins one way.

WHERE TWO RIVERS MEET

In Maine there was unspoiled land
as far as I could see,
beaches and cabins
sheltered by pine forests.

I had my first lobster
at a restaurant on a pier
with red and white checkered tablecloths.
I learned to skip flat stones,
perfect the glide across smooth water.

Today I'd like a quiet spot out there
where I can catch my own supper,
a private dock with a runabout.

It's funny how memories of childhood
become dreams in adulthood.

THOSE FINAL HOURS OF DAY

for Elaine

We'll never know
how many cakes Elaine frosted
for brides, expectant mothers, and families of faith;
one flawless day
they could each return to.

Her gift to family:
laughter and a grin
even on days overcast.

In early summer when we visited,
she and I marveled
at how the sun
touched fields and spun light
from the weathered roof of a cow barn,
quiet now
except for wind
whistling the metal bones of tractors.

We walked on in silence
through currents of wheat,
this was not the life we planned
but the one where we found each other.

STILL LIFE OF KOI

I hung the picture Sydney painted
for my 50th birthday,
then sat on the bed,
pondering the quandary of
such powerful fins
that splay only to glide over shiny coins,
tossed by strangers
in return for wishes,
but stripped of all value
in the shallow pool
where the Koi, deaf and unthinking,
can only repeat their circular, rhythmic paths.

Here's to another half-century.

THE END OF THE BEGINNING

Black and orange monarchs
dot the cool slate sky.
They will soon gift their color
to the autumn leaves,
surrender to something bigger.

CARRIE VOIGT SCHONHOFF draws inspiration for her writing from life in the Midwest that she shares with her two children and two Italian greyhounds. She lives between rural Wisconsin and the coast of North Carolina. This is her second collection of poetry.

ACKNOWLEDGEMENTS

The author wishes to thank family and friends who believed in this work from the beginning. She also wishes to acknowledge the friendship and editorial guidance of Simon Van Booy.